Ranches in the Southwest

by Cynthia Swain

Scott Foresman
is an imprint of

Glenview, Illinois • Boston, Massachusetts • Chandler, Arizona
Upper Saddle River, New Jersey

ISBN 13: 978-0-328-51639-1
ISBN 10:   0-328-51639-2

TABLE OF CONTENTS

Chapter 1 Southwestern Ranches

They sit high in the saddle on well-trained ranch horses. Who are they? Cowboys or cowgirls? **Dudes**? A dude is someone who grew up in the city but vacations on a ranch. Or are they helping ranchers do their work? Any of these is possible in the American Southwest.

Dude ranch guests take on cowboy duties.

Overgrazing damages the land.

Cowboys and cattle have been important to the ranches of the Southwest since the 1800s. Cattle provide the beef for the meat industry. But grazing, or putting cattle out to feed, causes problems. Cattle eat plants and make waterways dirty. They destroy plant growth. This endangers, or threatens, plant species and the animals that feed on them. As a result, the U.S. government may force ranchers to graze their cattle in different areas more often. This would cut down on overgrazing, which causes soil to be washed away.

Some ranches have failed because of these environmental factors. But many ranchers have changed their ranches. Some have taken on a new way of life, such as on a dude ranch. Other ranchers have kept their way of life by running a working ranch.

THE HORSE ADDS *Glamour* TO LIFE ON THE RANCHES...

Fly NORTHWEST AIRLINES TO THE HEART OF THE REAL DUDE RANCH COUNTRY

Horseback riding, as advertised in the 1940s, is one of the main activities on a dude ranch.

Chapter 2 Dude Ranches and Working Ranches

More than fifty years ago, some ranches began to take in guests. Today, dudes come from many parts of the world. These people are more used to urban, or city, life than to ranch life.

Dude ranches spend more time on guests than on cattle. They give horseback rides and lessons. Guests may also learn how to rope, or catch, cattle. Dude ranch owners work at making their guests comfortable.

Guests enjoy a barbecued meal at a dude ranch.

Some small working ranches also welcome guests. Working ranches and dude ranches both charge guests for their stay. But the focus of the working ranches is on taking care of cattle.

Guests at a working ranch, or guest ranch, usually know how to ride a horse. They come ready to work. Most guests want to feel what it is like to be a cowboy or cowgirl.

Many guest ranches like to offer a real ranch experience. They are often several hours away from a town. Some have no electricity, so guests must use lanterns. Lodging is usually in log cabins, which are comfortable but simple. The food is hearty and home-cooked.

These dude ranch guests may be ready to visit a working ranch after they have learned their roping skills.

Today, a roundup, or gathering of the cattle, is done almost the same way as it was a hundred years ago.

The guests bring in extra money for working ranch owners and make it possible for the rancher to keep running cattle. The visitors help gather up the cows and move them to grazing areas. Grazing away from river beds is better for the environment. It cuts down on contamination, or dirtying of the water. Extra help from guests means the cattle can be gathered and moved more often. Changing pasture lands also reduces damage to the environment.

Chapter 3 Life on a Ranch

Guest ranches are often found in the mountains. Winters are cold and snowy. Winter is not a rest period for ranchers. Days begin before dawn. Evening chores are not finished until about eight o'clock at night. In the winter, ranchers and their families take care of chores that do not require them to be out on the range. They may fix equipment or mend tack, such as a horse's saddle. They may fix fences and corrals near the ranch.

Roping is a good skill to have on a ranch.

In the winter, ranchers may gather up all their horses. They may spend some time training newer horses. Horses need to respond to a light touch of the reins or pressure on their sides. **Spurs** may be used to get a horse to pay attention.

In winter the cattle are left to graze on their own in a pasture. But feed must be taken to feeding stations on a regular basis, especially when it has been snowing.

A rancher working in the snow

Horses and their riders on a trail

The guest season lasts from May through October. It is a busy time on a guest ranch. The cattle must be gathered in what is called a roundup. They are brought in for cutting, sorting, branding, and any needed doctoring. *Cutting* means "singling out."

A lot of pastureland needs to be covered in a **roundup.** Ranchers hire extra help, such as horse wranglers, to care for horses, and cowboys, to care for horses and cows. Wranglers and cowboys, along with some guests, ride out in search of cattle and gather up any they find.

Guests also help with roping and branding, or marking of the cattle that belong to a certain ranch. The calves and cows that need to be branded are cut out from the rest of the herd. The sound of lowing cows and **bawling** calves that have been separated from their mothers mixes with the sound of guests helping to rope them. Guests learn that cooperation is needed to work on a ranch.

Guests help cowboys brand calves.

Nighttime on this ranch is peaceful and quiet.

During the summer, the crew moves groups of cattle to fresh pasture. To stay closer to the cattle, the crew, including guests, often stays out on the range at cow camps. Guests can sleep under the stars. They can fall asleep to–or be kept awake by–the sound of a **coyote** howling.

Ranches provide a range of experiences for visitors. Cowboys, cowgirls, dudes, and guests alike can enjoy the open spaces of the Southwest!

Glossary

bawling *v.* shouting or crying in a noisy way.

coyote *n.* a small, wolflike mammal living in many parts of North America.

dudes *n.* people raised in the city, especially easterners, who vacation on a ranch in the western parts of the United States and Canada.

roundup *n.* the act of driving or bringing cattle together from long distances.

spurs *n.* metal points or pointed wheels worn on riders' boot heels for urging horses on.

Reader Response

1. Reread page 5. What conclusions can you draw about cattle ranching and the environment?

2. Reread the chapter titles. How do they help you better understand the book? List each chapter title and below it write two interesting things you learned from that chapter.

3. Use a dictionary to find two meanings for the word *graze*. Write your response in a chart similar to the one below.

Word	Definition One	Definition Two

4. Reread page 14. What sights and sounds were part of the description?

Suggested levels for Guided Reading, DRA,™
Lexile,® and Reading Recovery™ are provided
in the Pearson Scott Foresman Leveling Guide.

Social Stud...

Genre	Comprehension Skills and Strategy	Text Features
Expository nonfiction	• Draw Conclusions • Graphic Sources • Text Structure	• Table of Contents • Captions • Glossary

Scott Foresman Reading Street 4.2.2

Scott Foresman
is an imprint of

ISBN-13: 978-0-328-51639-1
ISBN-10:   0-328-51639-2

9 780328 516391   90000 >

What It Takes to Stage a Play

by Leah Johnson

Vocabulary

advice

arguments

arrangements

descendant

dishonesty

script

snag

Word count: 769